# Life, in a Nutshell

Chris Brauer

 ISBN: 978-1-7773497-0-7

www.chrisbrauerwriter.com

# Author's Note

**I've been writing** a lot, lately – about all sorts of stuff.

I've been writing about walking mindfully through the old growth forests of British Columbia, and stopping to admire the magic and mystery of the natural world. I've been writing about finding joy in the little things that make up a day, and about being grateful for the guidance of all creatures great and small, and about the kindness of strangers. I've been writing love poetry.

But this book features very little of that. If you're into those kinds of things, you're welcome to read my musings on Facebook or buy my other books. Buy twelve, and you get the thirteenth for just one penny.

While I spend a significant portion of my day in quiet contemplation, I also spend much of it teaching elementary school, grocery shopping, hanging out with my wife and two sons, or just wandering aimlessly alone. And this is when all sorts of things happen to me. Not major, life-altering things. Funny things. Funny to me, anyway.

So I started writing them down in a brown leather journal I bought while strolling around Pike Place Market in Seattle. It's very nice.

*Life, in a Nutshell* is a diary, of sorts. Certainly not like the important diaries of Anne Frank and Samuel Pepys. More like the diaries of David Sedaris and Karl Pilkington.

While this little book (named after a song by Barenaked Ladies) is not a philosophical treatise, the fifty entries – anecdotes, observations, overheard conversation, jokes, memories – paint a picture of someone who constantly, against better judgment, approaches modern life with a certain amount of innocence and naivety.

I often catch myself whispering, "How hard can it be? What's the worst that could happen?"

Well... you're about to find out.

This is an introduction to my life – part of my life, anyway. It is the part that refuses to take itself too seriously.

I like laughing, and I like laughing at myself. There's a lot of that in here.

My students make me laugh, in a wonderful way. It's one of the main reasons I continue to teach after twenty years in the field.

Occasionally, I laugh at others. Stupid videos of

someone getting sacked by a baseball or a rogue golf club makes me chuckle. Perhaps that makes me a bit of a monster. Admittedly, there are times when I suffer from *schadenfreude* (the satisfaction or pleasure felt at someone else's misfortune) and I have to sulk back into my cave of shame. Sometimes I am culturally insensitive, and laugh at things like Chinese opera – *while* traveling in China. With a thousand teenagers.

I thought of leaving that part out, but I didn't. Despite popular opinion, I am not perfect. And I wanted to show that.

Though I can make a delicious butter chicken and clean the bathroom and fold laundry (minus the fitted sheets), I do have my faults.

I have always tried to find a sense of balance in my life. While I take what I *do* seriously, I try not to take *myself* too seriously. The words you are about to read will hopefully attest to that.

I think it's vitally important to find balance – to step back occasionally and see ourselves as the ridiculous creatures that we are. Stumbling through life. Pretending to know what we're doing.

*Life, in a Nutshell* is me, stepping back.

I initially thought that something silly isn't going to change anyone's life. That it's purely for fun.

But one never knows. Something as simple as a song, or a line of poetry, or even a collection of short sketches may just make all the difference in your day.

Writing is a solitary activity and, though social media does offer the opportunity for anyone to comment on various posts, it is always nice to hear from you. I may not have the time to respond to everything, but I will read everything.

Hunt me down. Tell me something funny that happened to you the other day or the other year. Laughing at yourself is harder than laughing at others, but it's ultimately far funnier. It's those kinds of stories that are best.

You may have noticed that this book is self-published. This worries me. The average self-published book sells very few copies. But I wanted to get this out in the world, and celebrate the lighter side of life.

Saying that, I would be enormously grateful if you'd spread the word or write a review. Write one if you think the book was worth the purchase. Write one if you didn't. That's okay. I like honesty.

I hope you enjoy *Life, in a Nutshell.*

# Life, in a Nutshell

I. **My wife and I** are approaching our mid-forties, and we noticed recently that some of our friends are 'getting old'. They're comfortable cruising through life, and see no reason to break away from their familiar patterns. They dress in the same clothes and have the same hairstyle since high school; they continue working the same job that they hate; they fly to the same holiday destination every summer; and they go to the same restaurant with the same group of friends every Friday night where they order the same thing. ("The usual?" the waitress asks. "You know it," they answer.)

In an effort to counter this state of cruise control, we've decided to do things that are outside our comfort zone. We'll start small – test the waters – and then, if that goes well, we'll start to do things that push us further. Who knows where this will take us? Maybe one day we'll go bungee jumping together in New Zealand. Or wear nothing but matching sequined booty shorts to Burning Man.

These tentative first few steps have included our time in the bedroom. It's nice that, after being married for almost fifteen years, we can still surprise each other behind closed doors. Just last night, for instance, I assumed that Paula was tired after a long day at work and, as I loaded the dishwasher, I expected that she would finish her glass of red wine and read from her Sherlock Holmes collection before falling asleep. But that isn't what happened.

Much to my surprise, I walked in to find that she had picked out her finest unmentionables. As I stood in the middle of the bedroom, she sashayed towards me with that sexy grin of hers that tells me she's up for something exciting. We awkwardly danced towards the bed, and then – in a breathy whisper – she told me to sit. "And enjoy the show."

I did as I was told, and my heart – as well as my imagination – began to race.

We maintained eye contact as she took a few steps back, her hips and shoulders seductively swaying from side to side.

And that's when my darling wife suddenly shrieked in disgust as she stepped in the cat's vomit that I failed to clean up before I left for work.

II. **My brother Ben** and my oldest son Adam are similar in many ways. They both prefer the city to the country; they both enjoy playing Dungeons & Dragons; and they both enjoy drinking craft beers at hipster bars with a highly tattooed staff. While I'm happy to sample a bacon-maple ale or a mango-jalapeño *gose* once or twice a year, I prefer a pint of Irish stout or a decent IPA.

While I have little desire to consistently 'nerd out' on craft beer, I will admit that lately I have been seeking out craft hot sauces. I have about a dozen bottles, with flavours like blueberry with scorpion peppers and black cherry with reaper peppers. Right now I'm slowly working my way through a product called Pain 100% from Kansas City. While the name isn't very inventive, I can't claim false advertising. It's warm, alright.

It may not be the hottest on the market, but it still packs a wallop and I use it sparingly on my burgers or scrambled eggs. Unfortunately, the sauce is on the thicker end and sometimes it's difficult to monitor the level of pain. Sometimes a big glob falls onto my plate and, rather than try to remove some of it, I just deal with the suffering.

This morning, as I was introducing long division to my class, there was a 'rumbly in my tumbly' and now I'm suddenly regretting my choice to add more hot sauce than I should have to my Campbell's mushroom soup the night before a teacher observation.

III. **My youngest son Nicholas** is always one step ahead of me when it comes to technology – which isn't difficult. It was only last year that I finally graduated from a flip-phone to an iPhone. When I became comfortable with that transition, he showed me the Spotify app and lately I've been exploring the radio option. I'll often stumble across songs I haven't heard in decades, and find others of a similar genre.

This morning, as I was unloading the dishwasher, I found the song "99 Luftballons" by German band Nena. After choosing the radio option, I thought that I would be treated to an array of one-hit wonders from the '80s. But instead I am now listening to German new wave synth-pop and moving my body in ways I never thought possible. Maybe I'm on to something here.

IV. **I got to play** a fun game this morning as I was running late for work: it's called 'Yogurt Container'. The aim is to find which yogurt container has the actual yogurt in it – not leftover spaghetti or mashed potatoes or chicken curry. It's very exciting!

V. **There are advantages** to living in town: I can walk to the pizza place, or the Indian restaurant, or the bookstore for a cappuccino. The grocery store is only a few blocks away. Most times I merrily return with a few bits and bobs, and continue on with my day. Occasionally, though, I underestimate the weight of certain items and my arms are a little sore by the time I enter the front door. I require a cup of tea to recover. Then there are times when I *grossly* underestimate the weight and have to huff and puff all the way home, whereupon I pour myself a stiff drink and watch an old James Bond film.

When my youngest son graduated from boy to young man (albeit a six-foot-two hulking brick shithouse of a young man), he needed a larger bed. But rather than pay for delivery of a new mattress, I had him assist me in walking it five blocks during the busiest time of the day. People honked. He wasn't impressed.

Then there was the incident with the Christmas tree.

There came a point when my wife was no longer interested in sweeping needles that were spread all over the house by the cats, or getting on her knees to water the damned things, or figuring out how to best dispose of them every January. But the real reason we finally opted for a fake tree was because of the time I attempted to heave a real one home, only to be laughed at by the local constabulary.

Like always, I approached the challenge with a

sense of childlike optimism. And for the first few minutes, I made decent progress. 'Easy peasy lemon squeezy,' I thought as I crossed the grocery store parking lot with my arms wrapped around it. 'Not a problem'.

But soon my arms started to ache and my fingers went numb. And that's when I had the brilliant idea to hook the string that was tied around the tree to my belt. I was redistributing the weight. 'Well done,' I thought. 'Gosh, I'm brilliant.'

About halfway, I was desperate for a break and was hoping to lean the tree against a building after unhooking the string from my belt. But there was a problem. I couldn't seem to unhook it. I was stuck to the tree. I thrust my hips from side to side, and jumped up and down. But no luck. Suddenly, I didn't feel so brilliant.

It was a quiet night, and there were no vehicles approaching, so I began to tussle with my adversary rather violently in hopes of untangling the string. I shook and shook. I may have said a nasty word. But to no avail.

And that's when I saw flashing red and blue lights reflected in the windows.

"How are you this evening?" asked the man in uniform.

"Um... pretty good," I answered – turning around to face him through the branches of the tree. "Lovely evening."

"Need any help, there?"

"Ah, no," I said. "I'm doing alright."

"You sure?" he asked as he waved his flashlight towards me.

"Sure, I'm sure."

"You wouldn't care for a police escort, would you? Wanna make sure you make it home safely." Then he started to laugh – *really* laugh. It was a full-on belly laugh. I thought he might hurt himself.

"No thanks," I said. I wish I could have seen the humour of the situation at that moment, but I was too embarrassed. Instead, I heaved the tree up and headed down the alleyway. Paula cut the string when I got home. She also laughed.

Since then, I never complain when I'm asked to haul the fake tree up the stairs from the basement.

VI. **I prefer running** in the woods, with no one around. I used to run from my house and along the highway, but I got tired of all the logging trucks kicking up dust and the teenage boys laughing hysterically as they swerved towards me. These days I am more likely to come across a deer or a moose or a bear than a human being, and that's okay by me.

Partly because there is no one around, and partly because I don't want to surprise any large woodland animals, I have taken to singing along to my favourite songs as I slowly make my way down winding country roads. I do this for nine months of the year.

In the winter, the roads are icy and covered with snow.

I tried those rubber traction devices that 'slip easily' onto one's shoes and feature a 'patented skid lock coil system', but I was still nervous that I'd slide off the road and into a ditch and have to holler for hours for help.

So for a few months every year, I reluctantly drag myself to the gym and continue my weekly runs on one of the four available treadmills.

I don't like running on treadmills. Even with music piped into my ears and three televisions tuned to different stations and a view overlooking the swimming pool, I get bored. It's just not the same. The time and distance flashes on the little screen, and there's zero chance of a nature encounter in the stale confines of the community complex.

Plus I have to change the way in which I run – that is to say I constantly have to remind myself *not* to sing along to my favourite songs. The compromise (if you can call it that) is to mouth the words instead.

Like grocery shopping, my motto when going to the gym is 'get in and get out'. Plug in, tune out, and get this done. But I was feeling surprisingly social today and, as I was changing into my outdoor shoes, I told an older lady about my struggles.

She listened intently and smiled when I was finished. "You know what?" she asked. "You know what I think?"

"No," I said as I looked up from my shoes. "What?"

"I think that... next time you're running on a treadmill, and you feel like singing, then you should just sing. You should just go for it."

I laughed as I finished lacing up my shoes and waved goodbye.

It was only as I was walking across the parking lot that I thought, 'Yeah... Maybe I will.'

VII. **I'm convinced** that my bellybutton collects far more lint than the average, but I have no evidence to back this up. Maybe I should start collecting data – weight, volume, however these things are done – and start asking others to do the same. Or is that weird?

VIII. **Nicholas is quickly approaching** his sixteenth birthday, and occasionally he goes in search of used cars. I talked to him today about how I learned to drive in downtown Victoria, and how maneuvering along the dark streets in the rain with the neon reflecting on the wet pavement and the windows fogging up was close to impossible for an inexperienced driver.

I also told him about when I was so excited to borrow my father's car for the first time that I forgot not just what level of the parkade I left the station wagon, but which parkade I had chosen. Want to know how long it takes to walk up and down all the parkades in downtown Victoria looking for a green station wagon with fake wood paneling? A long time.

IX. **A joke I heard:** A man calls his doctor and tells him to come over right away. "Please doctor," he pleads. "Please come quick. I think I'm going crazy."

"You understand that I don't normally do house calls?" says the doctor.

"I know... I know..." says the man. "But I'm begging you."

"I'll be over as soon as I can," says the doctor.

Fifteen minutes later, the doctor arrives at the man's house and rings the bell.

The man answers the door dressed in nothing but plastic wrap. "What do you think, doctor? Have I gone crazy, or what?"

The doctor looks the man up and down and calmly replies, "Well... I can clearly see you're nuts."

X. **Arming my entire class** with long sharp needles could only result in one of two options: either they make stunning works of fiber art, or they end up as human pincushions.

Some of my students find it difficult to keep their

water bottles balanced on the corner of their desks without knocking them over every few minutes, and I wondered if this was asking too much from them. I only had half a dozen Band-Aids in the first aid kit.

The janitorial staff would not be impressed if there were crisscrossing trails of blood from my room to the second-floor bathrooms, but I went ahead with the next unit in art class with optimism.

"Over the following couple weeks," I began, "you're going to be needle felting a small animal or a monster of your choosing and then a guest artist is coming to show us how to wet felt a forest floor. You'll not only learn about both styles of felting, but also about mindfulness. It's a painful reminder to stay in the moment when your mind wanders and you jab a needle into your thumb at full velocity."

Needle felting, I explained to my class, consists of using a sharp needle to turn wool roving into three-dimensional objects. Wool is agitated so that it sticks together, creating a solid fabric. Felting needles have very sharp barbs, and this is what helps agitate the wool.

"Poke straight up and down so that your needle comes in and out of the felt easily," I said. "It's okay if you break a needle, but there are ways to prevent it from happening too often. If you see the tip of your needle bend as you are poking it into your piece, this is an indicator that you are applying sideways pressure to your needle and it will snap. You can poke in and out at any angle as long as the tip of your needle stays straight."

"Um... Mr. Brauer..." interrupted one student.

"Yes? What's the matter?" I asked.

"I broke my needle while you were talking."

"But we haven't started yet, Julie."

"Yes, that's true," she said. "Can I have another one?"

I stroked my beard in pensive silence. "Yes, you can," I said. "But stop messing around. I don't have many extras."

Without any further interruptions, students began jabbing needles into coloured wool on top of foam pads. Everything was going well, when suddenly a hand shot up.

"Yes, John. Is there a problem?"

"Um... so... Maria broke her needle, and then she wanted to use mine, and then she borrowed mine for just a second, and then she broke that one too."

"That's super-awesome. So maybe Maria should just use her finger instead?"

"Does that work?" asked John.

"No," I replied. "It doesn't."

It was soon after that a horrible shriek cut through the classroom. The telltale drops of blood surfaced on the finger of one student, and then another. And then another. Some of the boys put on a brave face before running cold water over the tips of their fingers, while others tried to shake the pain away by flicking their wrists. Most of the girls quietly worked away, and were far less dramatic when they hit flesh instead of wool.

By the end of the hour, most students had the beginnings of something. A few students had what appeared to be a head and a body, while other projects looked as if they had melted in the sun like a bad candle. I tried to encourage all of them, but it wasn't easy and I had to hide my confusion as to what some projects were supposed to be.

"Is this good?" asked Sean.

"Yeah... that looks really good," I lied.

"You think so?"

"Oh, yeah. It's a really good...um..."

"It's a Pokémon."

"Of course. I knew that." This was also a lie. There is a lot of lying in teaching – though we usually call it positive reinforcement.

Most of the felting needles were broken by the end of the week (and I was soon out of Band-Aids), but we had a colourful collection of felt creatures in various states. Everyone is looking forward to wet felting next week.

Art class has been organized chaos, with wool roving spread across the school, and the students have been a lot louder than usual. But their enthusiasm is worth it. Success in the classroom can often be measured by the mess left behind at the end of the day.

XI. **After dragging the laundry basket** upstairs in the dark of a winter's morning, and sifting through my son's collection of black t-shirts, several pairs of jeans, and my impressive collection of themed boxer-briefs, I have now located seven socks. None of them match.

XII. **I met a woman today** who was looking after two ferrets. The man who bought the animals wanted to surprise his family on Christmas morning, and this kind individual had volunteered to watch them for a week and a half. I had to admit that I hadn't spent much time with ferrets.

"The last time I babysat a couple ferrets," she said, "one of them licked my eyebrow piercing, and then it got infected, and half my face blew up. It was crazy!"

"Wow," I said (mostly because I didn't know what else to say).

As I left the store, I thought, 'Well... there's another reason why *not* to get a piece of metal punched into my face.'

A ferret is still up for discussion.

XIII. **The more I travel,** the more I want to continue exploring far corners of the world and meeting new people. But if I'm being honest, I'm not good at traveling. While I like being there, I'm terrible at getting there. Something inevitably goes wrong – like the time I almost set fire to London Heathrow and then was kicked out for vagrancy.

Excited to settle in with my new laptop and watch several movies as I waited for my flight to Dubai, I tucked myself into a quiet corner. This was before comfortable airport charging stations, and I had to scan the walls looking for a place to plug it in. After twenty minutes, I finally found an outlet but I had to sit on a heating vent.

I am not an electrician (nor do I play one on television), but I knew that England used 230V power and Canada only used 120V power. This meant that if I wanted to use cheaper electrical devices from Canada while on my travels, I needed a convertor. For more expensive devices, I only needed an adapter because more expensive devices have a built-in convertor.

Unfortunately, jet lag made my head a little fuzzy. Rather than plugging my new laptop into an adapter, I instead plugged the expensive convertor into the wall, plugged my laptop into the convertor, and then turned on the power.

There soon followed a terrible crackling sound. 'That is the sound of bad things happening' I thought. 'Best not give myself away.'

This was soon after the transatlantic airline plot (to detonate liquid explosives) and I didn't want to be accused of terrorism. I tried to ignore the sound but everyone around me was standing up, hushing their children, and trying to find the culprit. That's when the smell of burning plastic filled the waiting area.

I knew I had to do something but I was panicking and sweating profusely. 'What the frig am I supposed to do now?' I asked myself, as I tried desperately to remain calm.

The rational side of my brain should have kicked in and I should have found the nearest airport employee. I should have explained what I had done. But, I didn't. Instead, when everyone else was looking the other way, I quickly slipped my laptop back into my bag and pulled the hot convertor out of the wall. Leaning over, and attempting to hide my face from security cameras, I found the nearest garbage bin and ditched the evidence.

In a panic and with no clear direction, I crossed the airport four times – back and forth, and back and forth again – in case there were any security agents trying to find me. After a couple hours, I settled down into a molded plastic chair, took a few deep breaths, and decided I had successfully escaped the authorities.

If I had been traveling with my family I would have booked a hotel room, as the layover was twenty-three mind-numbing hours. But, since I was traveling on my own, I thought I could save money and find a bench to sleep on. It wouldn't be a restful night, but I would be okay. I could sleep when I arrived.

It was shortly after 2:00am, as I was trying to get comfortable, that I noticed airport employees shutting down restaurants, cafés and gift shops. A few minutes later, there were only a few people left in the terminal and it was eerily quiet. 'That's weird' I thought. 'Surely these airport terminals are open twenty-four hours a day.'

If nothing else, I hoped that airport security would take pity on me and allow me to stay if I remained quiet and closed my eyes.

No such luck.

I soon felt a hand on my shoulder. "Sir, you can't stay here," said a lady in uniform.

"Really?" I asked.

"Yes, really," she said. "I'm afraid I have to accompany you through customs."

"I can't just sleep here until the terminal opens again?"

"No, you can't."

"I'll be quiet," I pleaded while swinging my legs off the bench.

"Sorry. The terminal closed half an hour ago."

She then led me through customs. Neither of us said anything further.

The man at customs was not amused. "Don't you have a place to stay?" he asked.

"No," I said. "I thought I could stay here for the night. My flight leaves tomorrow."

"You can't do that," he said. "The terminal closed half an hour ago."

He stamped my passport.

"Nice stamp," I said to lighten the mood. It didn't work.

The lady in uniform led me through the empty halls to the other side of security. "You can stay here for the night, if you want," she said, pointing me to the area between the main door and the security gates. "Security reopens at 6:00am."

"Okay," I said. "Thanks."

I didn't get any sleep that night.

XIV. **I was early** for a parent meeting this morning, so I visited the Grade 1 room. Students were at different stations after finishing their Language Arts worksheets, and one boy was playing with something called Plus-Plus. According to their website, it is described as 'one shape with endless possibilities'.

The boy was showing me how one could create a robot or a tiger, and I tried my best to make something resembling a dragon.

"Look," I said. "I made a dragon. What do you think?"

"Mmm..." he pondered. Then he looked up from the rug. "I think that next time you could do better."

XV. **With a ravenous teenager** in the house, it's not often that my wife and I get leftovers. But Nicholas had dinner at a friend's house and we happily dined on yesterday's *bibimbap*.

I was loading the dishwasher, and about to settle at my writing desk, when Paula asked if I'd like to go out for an order of hot wings and a pint or two of cider.

The bar wasn't empty or crowded, and there were just enough people (and enough noise) that we could have a nice conversation without feeling like anyone were listening in or that we had to shout at each other.

After forty-five minutes, and a couple drinks, our waitress asked us if we wanted another. My wife answered that we were going to head home soon and maybe finish off the night with a little tequila.

Our waitress smiled and her eyes lit up. "That sounds like fun," she said. And then she leaned over the table, so that she was only a few inches from my ear. In a breathy whisper she added, "I call tequila the naked maker."

My ears went red. I had no idea how to respond.

Paula laughed at me for the entire walk home.

XVI. **`It's an epidemic,`** I tell you. All over town, there are signs advertising GIFT'S in front of the jewelry store, HOT DRINK'S at the coffee shop, and POTATOES AND CARROT'S at the fruit stand.

Today I had an argument with a young woman at the liquor store. I was trying to calmly let her know that 6-PACK'S doesn't need an apostrophe.

"No... Six-packs... six-packs," she said as if I wasn't

even pronouncing it correctly and was new to the language.

"I understand how to say it," I said. "But you're pluralizing with an apostrophe."

She shook her head in disbelief and walked away.

I don't think I can consider this a 'win'.

XVII. **Rarely am I tempted** to purchase confectionery from the checkout aisle. Mints, maybe, for work – but that's about it. I'd be more tempted if the shelves were stocked with imported cheeses or sandwiches featuring spicy *capocollo* on dark rye with German mustard. That would be something.

If push came to shove, and I had to choose some kind of snack food, I would choose ketchup chips. For some reason, I like the odd chemical taste it leaves in the back of my throat.

When I took my youngest son to the corner store yesterday, I was going to stay in the car while he quickly picked up a bottle of root beer. Seamus Heaney's first collection of poetry had arrived in the mail and I wanted a few minutes to look it over.

"You can read later," said Nicholas. "Come in with me."

'Children are only children for a short amount of time,' I told myself, 'and one day he'll be asking me to stay in the car while he runs in with his friends'.

"Alright," I said. "I'm coming."

Inside, we stared at the cooler full of craft sodas and I found a bottle of sarsaparilla. "I haven't seen sarsaparilla since I was your age," I said.

"What is sarsaparilla?" asked Nicholas.

"Actually, I don't really know. But it kind of tastes like root beer."

As I stared at the bottles of orange soda and cherry cola, I was transported back to my youth – a time when I spent my allowance on one of two things: either video games or candy.

And that's when I turned around and found a little box of Nerds.

"I didn't know they still made this stuff," I said. "What responsible parent allows their children to eat this crap?"

"I'm hoping that's you... today... right now," replied Nicholas.

Looking down at the Fun Dip and Pixy Stix and Pop Rocks, I knew there was no other option. "There really is no other option," I said, "but to buy a ridiculous amount of candy."

I bought all of the above and more: Runts and Gobstoppers and something I'd never heard of called Toxic Waste.

"Those are really sour," warned Nicholas.

"Really, *really* sour?" I asked.

"Yes. Just have one at a time."

I ignored his advice and had three. He was right. They were really sour. My salivary glands protested and there were tears in my eyes and, after the pain subsisted, I ate three more before moving on to something less abusive.

It didn't take long for either of us to feel the effects of the sugar rush. We were talking twice as fast as we normally would, and I suddenly had the urge to go for a long run or to vacuum an entire apartment complex.

By late afternoon, I wasn't feeling very well. "I think I'm going to lie down for a few minutes," I said.

"Me too," said Nicholas.

When my wife came home from work just before dinnertime, I confessed what I had done. "This is not my best parenting moment," I said.

"Have either one of you had any real food today?" she asked.

"We had cereal for breakfast," I said as I groaned.

"I'm going to make dinner," said Paula as she shook her head in disbelief. "Maybe that'll help."

After a hearty bowl of soup and fresh bread, I spent the rest of the evening watching Netflix in bed.

I still didn't feel well this morning as I woke up.

"I feel pretty rough," I said.

"You have a sugar hangover," said my wife.

"What? Is that even a thing?" I asked.

"Yes, it is."

"Well... that's just stupid," I said.

"Yeah... Speaking of stupid..."

XVIII. **While "Horse With No Name"** is arguably catchy, the lyrics penned by 1970s folk-rock band America are nonsensical to the point of ridiculousness. The pinnacle of this absurdity culminates at the line "the heat was hot".

'Of course the heat is hot', I thought today as I looked for some obscure item in the grocery store that my wife added to the list at the last second.

But then I thought of my time in Beijing. While I had experienced summer months in hot places – the Yucatan Peninsula, the Arabian Desert, and the streets Hong Kong – Beijing in July is a different sort of beast. Nothing can prepare one for the smoggy, humid heat that burns like a chemical sauna (much like ketchup chips).

I arrived in the middle of the night with forty-three high school students and four other teachers from across British Columbia. The first day of the international summer camp hosted by the Chinese government was to begin in less than six hours and, by the time we did a head count, collected everyone's luggage from the turnstile and boarded the bus, we were all ready for bed.

But an eager college student was waiting at the gates, ready to take us on a tour of the dark hallways and expansive courtyards. So, in a haze of exhaustion, we shuffled around for almost an hour.

After all the students had found their bunks, and I collapsed into my single bed, I wasn't concerned about the heat or humidity or blanket of smog. The only thing on my mind was the 5:30am wake-up call.

I am not at my best when forced to operate on four hours of sleep within a forty-eight hour period, but I managed to drag myself into the shower before stumbling into the enormous cafeteria. I mindlessly shoveled something resembling food into my face and then boarded a tour bus where I watched an hour of the sprawling city go by in the rising daylight.

We arrived at the Beijing Garden Expo Park, along with twenty-six other busses – loaded with twelve hundred students, teachers, tour guides and other staff. As I exited the air-conditioned bus, I was instantly uncomfortable. I found it hard to breathe or even think. My assigned blue camp T-shirt was two sizes too small, and that didn't help. I looked like a poorly aged superhero.

Once everyone had unloaded, we hiked up the steep hill. The heat had such intensity that we all struggled to keep upright. Some kid started whistling the theme to *The Bridge on the River Kwai*. I would have laughed if I weren't so knackered. Everything seemed out of focus and I wondered if the soles of my shoes would melt if I didn't keep moving. When we finally crested the ridge and found the long wooden benches in the grass at the outdoor auditorium, we collapsed in tangled heaps like clocks in a Salvador Dalí painting.

After a long delay, the opening ceremonies finally began and we all perked up. The first half-hour featured various groups of young women playing folk songs on traditional instruments, and we politely applauded after each song. Then it was time for Chinese opera. This was distinctly unpleasing. It sounded like someone torturing a herd of goats by shoving them into a wood chipper. I almost forgot about the heat.

When the government officials made their grand entrance, the heat seemed doubly unbearable. A convoy of golf carts rolled into view, loud orchestral music boomed from the speakers, and the camera crew leapt to their feet. We were all encouraged to clap enthusiastically as each official took to the stage. Over the next half-hour, each one stepped up to the microphone (with translator) and welcomed us to China before opening the camp.

The official flag and official T-shirt were presented (even though we were all wearing them), and then various men and women in business suits shook each other's hands. Suddenly, like waking from a bad dream, it was all over and we headed back down the hill.

We were hoping to find tour busses waiting for us, with comfy seats and air-conditioning, but there were none. Instead, we were led around the outer ring of the park without any hint of what we were looking at, where we were going, or when this madness might end. Some students took photographs of pagodas through the smog, but most just stared down at their feet.

Our group stopped for a bathroom break when, all of a sudden, someone spotted an ice cream stand. "Ice cream! Ice cream!" and suddenly fifty-four teenagers and three teachers ran across the grass waving *yuan* in their desperate fists. It was a special kind of chaos.

Only half the group managed to buy a frozen treat before the wide-eyed vendor was sold out. With bitter disappointment in their overheated hearts, those still in line turned their backs on temporary salvation and marched on. I almost felt bad as I bit into my ice cream and chocolate sauce dripped down my chin.

About twenty minutes later, we found another snack bar and everyone was given ample time to buy something to quench their thirst and cool their internal body temperature. I imagined these brave teens had never experienced joy like this before, but were also wondering why on earth they signed up for any of this.

Soon after, we heard the distant blaring of Chinese pop music. I thought at first that someone's cell phone was ringing, but a small crowd started to gather on the edge of the ring road. The music got louder and louder as more people gathered. I looked to our tour guide to see if he knew what was going on, but he just shrugged his shoulders.

As the first few parade floats went by, it looked like some sort of fashion show. Young ladies were waving flags or twirling like Disney princesses. Then it dawned on me that the whole spectacle was meant to highlight China's heroic past and triumphant future. It assured all attendees – in sensory overload – that China always has and always will be glorious. When the parade ended and the crowd broke off, I just stood in awe.

I can't remember how far we had to walk to find the busses. I only remember wondering how the rest of my time in Beijing was going to unfold. I also remember looking up to where the sun was trying to bust through the impenetrable pollution and unconsciously humming, "The heat was hot..."

XIX. **Today was one** of those days when I had to explain that I'm not Christmas shopping in my shorts because I'm some sort of tough guy, but because I accidently threw all my pants in the laundry half an hour ago. My legs are so white. It's embarrassing.

XX. **Overheard** at the staff Christmas party: "Oooh... a cheese ball. I like cheese, and I like balls!"

XXI. **I was hoping to work** on a new poem today. It's been about three weeks since I've sat down to focus on extended metaphors and the such, and I made sure to go through all my rituals: I lit some sandalwood incense; I poured myself some strong black coffee; and I found an early recording of Gregorian chants on vinyl. I was making decent progress, and tapping into the flow of the universe, when I noticed that the music had stopped.

I got up to flip the record and, lo and behold, the damned cat stole my chair. Now I'm sitting at the dining room table, but it's just not the same. I know what you're thinking, but she looks so peaceful, curled up and lightly snoring. Maybe if I empty the dishwasher and fold some laundry, she'll have moved.

*UPDATE: No such luck. I assume she'll be there all day. Maybe I'll write in bed.*

XXII. **I bought a new bathing suit** today that features sloths: sloths doing yoga, sloths on unicycles, sloths surfing. The previous one has lasted me since I had returned from living in the Sultanate of Oman – some twelve years. Our time there was as much about living in a foreign land and being a cultural minority as it was trying to navigate parenthood. And the silly sloths reminded me of spending lazy afternoons at the local resort in the southern city of Salalah.

The lower pool featured a rock wall. Though the pool manager didn't like it, expat children often climbed up the wall and rolled over the top to the bar pool. I thought that climbing up with Adam on my back would be a fun challenge.

"Hey, Adam! Climb on my back."

"Why?" he asked.

"Because I want to pretend I'm Luke Skywalker and you're Yoda."

"Okay," he said, excitedly.

It was only ten feet from the surface of the water to the ledge of the bar pool, but we imagined it taller. With its rough surface and easy footholds, the wall didn't make for a significant challenge and I was feeling confident we could make it to the top.

I was only halfway when Adam started to slip. His fingers dug into me, but it was no use. I wasn't concerned about his safety, as he would just fall to the water below, but I still felt that I should reassure him. "Adam, are you okay back there?"

"I'm slipping," he said.

"We're almost there," I said.

"We're not going to make it."

"Just hang on," I said. I found another foothold and heaved up the wall a few more inches. I was searching for a handhold when he slipped further down.

He began to pull on my shorts. "This is it," he said. "This is the end."

"No, Adam. We can make it."

"Tell my mother that I love her." He then pulled hard on my shorts. They fell to my ankles.

"Shield your eyes!" I heard Adam yell just before he hit the water.

I jumped in quickly and pulled my shorts up, hoping no one had seen me. Adam decided he would rather go down the yellow waterslide than try again.

"That's probably for the best," I said.

XXIII. **The royal family** was not part of my upbringing – we had no commemorative plates or spoons or whatever it is that royalists collect – but I've spent the last few days binge-watching the latest season of *The Crown* on Netflix. Every five or ten minutes, I have to pause the show to research the events that are highlighted or find out what the characters looked like in real life. This means that it takes me twice (or three times) as long to watch each episode than most people, but I'm in no rush.

Right now, I'm sitting up in bed with my laptop and eating a snack to avoid working on report cards. It's difficult to concentrate when I have to type, for the eleventh time, something along the lines of, 'David needs to read the questions on the math tests more carefully so as not to make silly mistakes. But have a wonderful holiday season. And see you in the new year!'

The thing is, after watching four episodes back-to-back, I now have to fight the urge to rewrite every term comment in the Queen's English.

XXIV. **I decided today** that I'd do more yoga if the floor weren't so far down.

XXV. **Similar** to 'Pile of Laundry', in which players can place bets as to who will finally collect the ever-growing mountain and move it into the laundry basket, 'Dishwasher' also has a similar feel. This time the question is who will finally empty the machine.

In the blue corner is the teenage son who has been politely asked five times within the last hour, and in the red corner is the frustrated father who should count his losses, crank a classic Pearl Jam song, and just get it done.

XXVI. **Our alarm code** at the school changed over the holiday, and we all received an email informing us of the new number. I hope it follows a certain pattern, or there's no chance that I'll remember it.

This made me think of the time I was substitute teaching at a two-room rural school tucked into the woods and had to wait for the police to show up as I sat outside on the steps one chilly winter morning. I was sure I knew the alarm code then, but it turns out that I was wrong.

I had taught part-time there years earlier, and was confident that all would be well when I picked up the key en route.

"Do you need the alarm code?" asked the nice lady behind the desk.

"No," I said quickly. "I've got one. Not to worry."

It only occurred to me twenty minutes into my drive that the code I had been given three years previously may have changed. 'Ah... I'm probably fine,' I thought. 'What's the worst that could happen?'

Mine was the only car in the small parking lot. Though an educational assistant was due to arrive before school started, I had left early so I had time to look over the day-plan and leisurely enjoy my morning coffee.

I walked up the wooden steps to the front door, unlocked it, and heard the familiar staccato tweet from the alarm system that reminded me I had three minutes in which to punch in the appropriate four-number code.

That's when I realized I had forgotten where the security keypad was located. It wasn't near the front door, and I frantically searched up and down the short hallway. I looked inside the office. Time was quickly ticking away.

After two minutes that felt nothing like two minutes, I finally found the keypad behind a small locked metal panel. Luckily, the same key that unlocked the front door unlocked the metal panel, and I had just enough time to punch in four numbers.

I was expecting a quick beep to confirm that my code was valid and I could continue on with my day. But there was no quick beep. I tried again, but again there was no quick beep. I tried a third time – still no beep. That's when my three minutes were up and a loud shrieking filled the quiet.

"That's not good," I said to myself as I broke into a sweat. "What do I do now?"

A faded sticker on the inside of the metal panel read: 'If you have accidently set off the alarm, please call...'

The noise was so intense that I decided to quickly copy the number into my cell phone and head outside, rather than use the phone in the office.

I walked down the wooden steps and into the parking lot before dialing. But my cell phone didn't appear to be working. Much to my surprise, there was no signal. "Dang it," I said. "That's not going to work."

I turned around, went back up the steps and tried the front door. The door was locked. I checked my pockets for the key. No key. I checked my pockets again. Still, no key.

Peering through the front door window, I could just make out the keys hanging from the metal panel. "Double dang it."

I had no other option but to sit on the steps and wait for the police to arrive. Feeling restless and a little nervous – not to mention embarrassed – I paced around the parking lot. I wasn't sure how I was going to explain what I had done to the first attending officer.

It wasn't long before a white cruiser could be seen through the thin bushes that separate the rural road from the highway.

"Well... that didn't take long."

But the cruiser didn't turn off the highway, cross the tracks, and drive towards the school. It just drove past and kept on its way.

Soon after, the alarm turned off. I don't know why. And a few minutes later, a staff member arrived. I explained what I had done.

"If you don't tell anyone, then I won't either," she said.

That afternoon, a handyman arrived and started tinkering with the keypad. He looked confused. "Did you notice anything strange this morning with the alarm system?" he asked me.

"No," I answered. "Nothing that I know about."

XXVII. **I bought a new** laundry basket today, and then decided to walk home with it over my head like a medieval knight.

This is how one entertains one's self in a small town.

XXVIII. **We have two cats.** Molly enjoys the outside and socializing in the daytime with hair salon clients downstairs in Paula's shop. Bella enjoys the inside and socializing in the evening with her family.

Molly is gentle; Bella seems to enjoy the act of drawing blood when she's in one of her moods.

I was thinking about the differences in our cats this morning as I was picking out a pair of X-Men underwear (as one does), and I thought back to when I was sitting on the edge of the bed inspecting my vasectomy stitches.

With my back turned to the door, I looked down between my legs and wondered how difficult it would be to just pull the tiny knot through the hole. Surely, a quick tug should do the trick. And I could avoid another awkward visit to the doctor's office.

These are the kinds of things that cause one to be fully engrossed, and I was unaware of anything else. No other thoughts competed for space. No pop songs played in my head. Which is why I failed to hear (or even sense) Bella walking into the room.

Another difference between the two cats is that – even though both are smaller in stature – Molly is heavy-footed, whereas Bella is ninja-like in her movements. And so, I had no inkling that Bella was directly beside me. Until it was too late.

I was carefully pulling the surgical thread back and forth – still wondering if at-home stitch removal was a good idea – when I pondered my tolerance for pain. 'I've experienced higher levels of pain,' I thought. 'I've had several tattoos; I've whacked the top of my head on the hatch of a car; Adam once rammed a luggage cart into my Achilles' heal in the Dubai airport. This shouldn't be *that* bad.'

And that's when Bella swung. And made full contact. Meaning, she didn't just slice my tender testicle. She hooked in. And pulled.

And suddenly my experience of pain hit a new high.

So did my voice. I wasn't aware I could shriek so loudly.

Since then, if anyone ever asks me about the worst pain I have ever felt, I know exactly which story I'm going to tell – but it requires a stiff drink.

XXIX. **Me: Do you want** me to put on some music?

Paula: Yeah, okay.

Me: What would you like?

Paula: It doesn't matter.

Me: Yeah, it does.

Paula: Okay, it does. It's Sunday morning. I'm enjoying my coffee and reading my book. Don't put on your friggin' Irish marching tunes.

Me: Ha-ha-ha.

XXX. **My car had a funny smell** today, so I did what any logical person would do: I pulled over, adjusted my baseball cap, and kicked a tire in hopes that the problem would magically fix itself.

I must have the special touch, because the smell soon dissipated.

A little further down the road, as I was eating Flamin' Hot Cheetos with one hand and steering with the thumb of another, I suddenly remembered the time I almost killed my younger brother with a car tire. And I laughed.

And then I wondered if Ben thinks about all the adventures and misadventures – the things we got away with and some of the things we didn't – as we grew up in the suburbs of Victoria. I wonder if he occasionally smiles at the memories, marveling at how we both survived. I should probably ask him one day.

I wonder if he remembers games of extreme bike tag around the neighbourhood and the time I thumped him and sent him into a parked car, busting off the driver side mirror. I wonder if he remembers being talked into roller-skating through the shopping mall and being chased by security. I wonder if he remembers when I ninja-kicked him off a friend's trampoline. He landed on the root of a tree and needed several chiropractic treatments. (I bet he remembers that.)

I'm not sure if Ben remembers the incident with the car tire, or if he remembers it as vividly as I do, but for me it was a defining moment for both of us.

We grew up across the street from a large forested park, and spent countless hours exploring the lesser-known trails with Baggins (our English Cocker Spaniel) when we weren't having water balloon fights in our bare feet or playing night-tag with flashlights. Sometimes we took advantage of our steep driveway. As the house was below street level, we transformed it into a dangerous sled run that abruptly ended at the garage door on the rare occasion it snowed. It also meant that all the groceries, camping gear, decorative rocks, and anything else our parents made us haul had to be heaved up and down the front lawn.

Like most children of the 1980s, we spent Saturday mornings watching cartoons and enjoying our small allotment of sugary cereal. We were allowed two or three television programs before being sent outside, but often we'd get lucky. If we were quiet, we could get away with 'frying our eyes and rotting our brains' until lunchtime. At some point, however, my mother grew frustrated at having to constantly remind us to turn the damned thing off. She'd walk over and yank the plug out of the wall.

On one particular morning, we were sent out to 'help' our father change a car tire. We weren't expected to actually do anything but merely stand around, looking a little goofy with our hands in our pockets. This was more about keeping us busy and away from the television than actually making any real contribution. Somehow the experience of being there, as our father got his hands dirty and swore under his breath, was touted as male bonding and we reluctantly headed up the front lawn.

Neither Ben nor I had any experience with car tires, but my father eventually bestowed the responsibility to us of wheeling the old tire (rim and all) down the driveway and into the garage. It was an easy enough task, my father assumed, even though it had some heft to it.

My father went inside for a snack and to catch the hourly news on the radio, and it was up to me (being the eldest) to oversee the project.

I wanted to appear as if I were in charge so, before embarking on what should have been an easy task of carefully inching the old tire down the driveway, I took a moment to reassess the situation.

It occurred to me, as a soft breeze ruffled my hair, that there might be a more effective way to get the job done. The faster we finished, the sooner we could talk our mother into watching more television. An episode of *He-Man and Masters of the Universe* was starting soon and I didn't want to miss it.

And that's when brilliance struck – or so I thought.

My plan would not involve putting my tender ten-year-old body at risk, but that of my brother (two years my junior). And with misplaced confidence, I sent Ben down the driveway to the open garage. Had I considered physics or human biology, I would have realized that my idea was a bad idea. But I was only thinking of myself.

Begrudgingly, Ben headed down the driveway and turned around to face me. I had him shuffle a bit to the left and then to the right, so that he was dead centre in the middle of the open garage. Satisfied that he was exactly in line with me, and closing one eye to aim, I then pushed the tire down the driveway.

As the tire picked up speed, I nodded in a self-congratulatory way. 'Well done,' I thought. '*He-Man*, here I come.'

Only when the tire neared the halfway mark, did I suddenly realize that maybe this was a bad idea. As Ben stood with his arms outstretched – like some sacrificial offering – and the tire rushed faster and faster on its trajectory of death, I imagined the rest of my life as an only child.

There was no time to yell or to scream – and no time to run after the damned thing. I could only watch in terror as time slowed down and the fabric of space tore open.

Then something I can't quite explain happened. Perhaps it was some force from beyond. Perhaps it was the work of angels or faeries or little green men from another planet. Or perhaps it was just luck.

As the tire neared the end of the driveway, it wobbled ever so slightly. And, rather than hitting Ben and possibly killing him, it hit the door next to the garage. Actually, it didn't just hit the door; it blew the door off its hinges.

I was relieved that the tire had not crushed my brother but I knew, as the door hit the back of the garage and the noise echoed down the street, that my parents would soon be storming out of the house and demanding to know what had occurred.

And that's exactly what happened. My brother

had no interest in covering for me, and revealed my terrible plan. I was grounded. No *He-Man,* or any other television, for an entire month. I felt it best not to argue.

Years have passed. Ben now works for an engineering firm in Vancouver, where he buries himself in complex numbers and science. I'm an elementary teacher in a small town, and do my best to avoid complex numbers and science.

We haven't looked back since.

XXXI. **Kingfisher Used Books** & Fine Coffee is located only two doors up the street from where I live. I've nipped up there in my socks for a mid-afternoon cappuccino; I've fallen asleep on the couch; and I've squirreled away novels in random corners when I've forgotten my wallet. The owners – Joe and Katherine – sometimes put books aside that they think I might enjoy. I finished one such book today called *Mortification: Writers' Stories of Their Public Shame.*

Edited by Robin Robertson, the book features vignettes of various length by over seventy contributors. These stories made me laugh, and squirm, and come to terms that "a writer's public life... is, in fact, a grim treadmill of humiliation and neglect."

It also made me think of my own story of mortification.

It happened when I worked as the editor of a local

newspaper, and was asked by the facilities manager of a nearby seniors' home to read some of my work.

"An hour would be great," she said. "The residents would love to hear some of your stories. We just had the mayor in this week, and some gentleman with a guitar."

"Okay," I said. "I guess that'll be fine." I was trying to convince myself as much as anything else.

I had only read once before in public when I nervously mumbled my way through a few pages before sitting down, vowing never to do that again in the near future. And yet here I was – standing at a tall lectern, and sharing a small room with twenty seniors and three standing fans.

I know now that an hour is a *really* long time to be with an audience. Most readings I've been to lately have included an introduction by the host, some music, and a question-and-answer period – and wrap up before an hour is done. And that's with an audience whose average age is less than eighty-six years.

Still, I approached the lectern with my papers and introduced myself before reading from my travel memoir about Oman. It didn't occur to me that perhaps no one in the room had ever heard of the obscure Middle Eastern country – or even cared – but I kept at it for what seemed like forever.

When I got to the end of the first chapter, I looked at my phone. I was hoping my time was up. But this was not the case. However, I had put five audience members to sleep.

“Does anyone have any questions?” I asked to those whose eyes were still open.

There were no questions.

“Any comments? Anything?”

A hand shot up.

“Yes... the gentleman in the back.”

With a strained grunt and a loud snort, the gentleman in the back stood up, and I prepared myself for a question about the writing process or what I had experienced living and teaching in the sultanate.

“You know what I zink?” he asked in a thick German accent.

“No,” I answered. “What?”

“I zink zat zee interviews you do for zee paper are good. But I zink your writing is BORING!”

“Oh,” I said. That’s...um...well...” I had no idea how to respond as I scanned the room. “Any other questions or comments?”

Somehow I made it through another half-hour, and thanked my audience for listening. In a blur, I packed up my papers and power-walked down the hall, out the front door, and across the parking lot to my car. My only hope was that the mayor did worse.

XXXII. **We dropped my son Adam** and his girlfriend Jane off at the airport this morning for their flight to Vancouver. The queue for security was long and, as we said goodbye, I was reminded of the last time I flew to the big city for a teachers' conference.

I was seated next to a woman I didn't know, and was planning to plug into my phone and be antisocial.

But the woman kept chatting and chatting and chatting.

She was also a teacher but, unlike me, she was terrified of flying.

"I find it helps to talk with the person sitting next me," she said.

"Oh, right," I said. "Well... I guess that's me."

She chatted non-stop through take-off and, as we were approaching cruising altitude, I felt that this was going to be one of the longest flights ever.

Then I watched in utter amazement as she pulled six mini bottles of vodka from her purse.

"If you ask the flight attendant for a couple orange juices," she said, "we can have screwdrivers."

Suddenly the flight didn't seem too bad.

"Sounds good," I said, peering behind me at the snack cart and lowering my tray table.

XXXIII. **According to Wikipedia,** "early use of the phrase 'Netflix and chill' was without sexual connotations, referring simply to the act of watching the online streaming service, typically by oneself."

If one did not know that the term had evolved beyond this 'early use' and has since taken on a euphemistic nature, then one might say something embarrassing – something along the lines of, "Goodnight Nicholas. Sleep well. Your dad and I are going to Netflix and chill."

I could hear my son laughing from down the hall. "I don't think that means what you think it means."

*NOTE: Apparently, Disney+ and thrust is also a thing.*

XXXIV. **In a brave attempt** to bond with my son over video games, I found myself completely out of place. This was a world I left behind a long time ago, and didn't think I'd ever return.

"Back in my day," I began, "most video games only required two buttons. 'A' was punch and 'B' was jump. And that's it."

I knew as soon as the words left my mouth that I sounded old.

But I continued. "Now there's a billion different buttons or combinations of buttons, and I can't remember *anything*."

"I'll guide you through," said Nicholas.

"I'll be dead in no time," I said.

"I have faith in you."

Despite his encouragement, I ended up whacking the controller and hoping for the best every time the action got too intense. After trying my hand at *Overwatch* (and being cyber-bullied for sucking so bad), I tried a Star Wars game called *Battlefront II*. I got shot in the exact same spot fourteen times, so I gave up and made us both tea.

XXXV. **Ideally, I'd show up** to the gym and there'd no one there. But right now, it's that awkward period between Christmas and New Year's when everyone wants to get a jump on their resolutions. There were dozens of people. DOZENS! And all the treadmills were being used by people walking. WALKING! I mean, what the hell?

XXXVI. **Eating better** has constantly topped my list of New Year's resolutions. That, and going to the gym more than once every two weeks. It was only the other day that I asked myself, 'Is there any way in which macaroni and cheese can be considered a vegetable?' According to my wife, the answer is 'no'.

XXXVII. **'How hard can it be?'** has become my new mantra this year. Well... it turns out that there are plenty of things that are hard. Eating celery is one. It's like the jellyfish of the vegetable kingdom: mostly water and string. Why bother? In soups and stews are fine (I guess), but raw celery is just weird.

XXXVIII. **My boys aren't young** anymore. Neither come to me looking for Band-Aids when they have an owie, or a glass of milk before bedtime.

Sometimes I miss those days. I come across artwork that Paula has saved from when they were in kindergarten, or books that we read to them night after night after night, and I have to fight to hold back a tear or two.

But then I re-read some journal entries from our time in Oman, and suddenly the raw truth comes rushing back.

One thing I don't miss is finding an appropriate place to eat in a foreign country, when we're all tired and cranky and no one is interested in spending another minute in a mega-mall full of noise and lights.

After weaving through a couple pink aisles and expensive themed LEGO sets at Toys 'R' Us, Adam finally spent some of his own money on a foam sword that made a satisfying *thwack* when it hit bare flesh. I bought one for myself too. And one for Nicholas.

As the boys and I fought with swords in the underground parking lot, Paula asked the age-old question that has haunted vacationing families through the ages: "Where are we eating tonight?"

"I don't know," I said, dodging a sword to the head.

"There's a seafood restaurant next to Starbucks. It's not too far from here, and it's the only place I can think of right now."

"Maybe you could think clearer if you weren't sword fighting."

"Maybe," I said. "But where's the fun in that?"

It wasn't difficult to find the restaurant, and we were soon seated with menus in hand. The prices were higher than we expected, but we were on holiday. We clinked our water glasses and settled in for a relaxing meal.

Soon after the waitress took our order, Adam needed to use the washroom. He was old enough to use the facilities on his own, and we pointed him downstairs. Five minutes went by and we thought nothing of it. Five more minutes went by, and we assumed Adam was deep in thought and had lost track of time. Another five minutes went by.

"Please go check on him," said Paula.

"I'm sure he's just lost in La-La Land," I said.

"Take Nicholas. He's restless and a short walk might do him good."

"A short walk to the bathroom?"

"Please."

"Fine, I'll go."

I took Nicholas by the hand and we went downstairs to check on Adam. As we walked into the men's washroom, we heard muffled cries for help. Adam had locked himself in a bathroom stall and couldn't figure out how to unlock the double-lock. In an attempt to unlock the stall, he had locked it twice.

"Adam, is that you?" I asked.

"Yes," he squeaked.

"What's the matter?"

"I can't get out. It wouldn't unlock. You need to find a key."

"Alright," I told Adam. "Just relax. I'll be right back."

I headed upstairs with Nicholas to find someone that could help.

A young Thai waitress was sorting cutlery near the back of the restaurant. "Hello," I said.

"Yes. Can I help you, sir?"

"My son has locked himself in a bathroom stall. Is there a key or something?"

"Um, no sir. No key. It is double-lock. Click-click," she said and mimicked unlocking the door.

"Oh," I said. "Okay."

We found Adam where we had left him. He was crying.

"Get me out of here!" he yelled.

"Okay, listen. There's no key."

"What!? Oh, no," he sobbed. "I can't fit under the door. I already tried. I'm going to be stuck here until I die."

"Probably," I answered.

That wasn't the best reply. Adam wailed.

I felt bad. "Listen," I said slowly, "the lock is a double-lock. You need to turn it twice to the right."

There was silence as Adam tried to turn the lock. He took a deep breath but, defeated, announced, "It just won't turn."

"Try the other way."

"I can't. My hands are sweaty."

"Wipe them off. Our dinner is probably on the table." I was hungry, Nicholas was pulling on my leg, and my patience was wearing thin.

"I can't do it. It's over," he repeated.

"Relax, Adam," I said, trying to sound calm. "Try again. It's not over. Just calm down and try again."

I waited for a little while longer, but Nicholas was hungry and wanting to join his mother. "Adam, I'm going to take your brother back upstairs. Keep working on the lock."

"Okay," he answered feebly.

Dinner was quickly getting cold. I explained what was happening in the bathroom and told Paula to start. "I'm going back down to check on Adam," I said. "Try to get Nicholas to eat something."

Adam was standing outside the stall, looking relieved.

"I figured it out," was all he could say.

We returned to the table to find Paula finishing her plate and Nicholas picking away at his. Adam and I dived in.

"I'm going to take the little one for a walk," said Paula, "before he escapes."

"This isn't the nice, relaxing meal I was hoping for," I said.

"I know it isn't. Maybe one day... " trailed Paula as she headed outside.

As Adam finished his dinner, I had the rest of Nicholas' food boxed up, though I had my doubts as to whether he would eat any of it later.

I was desperate to leave, but I couldn't find our waitress. The restaurant had filled up and we were being ignored. I searched the entire place as Adam stared off into space.

Frustrated with bathroom stalls, stubborn children, overpriced lukewarm dinners and disappearing staff, we drove back to our hotel.

I lay in bed, ready to slip into blissful slumber.

"Are you asleep already?" asked Paula.

"No," I answered. "I'm just resting my eyes."

"I don't think the boys have had enough to eat."

"That's too bad," I said. "But that's their problem; not mine."

"I need you to do something about it."

"Point them down the road. Maybe they'll come back. Maybe they won't."

Paula leaned over me. "*Please...*"

"Fine," I said, struggling to right myself. "I'll walk down the road a bit and see what I can find."

"Thank you."

I stepped out into the warm night, so exhausted I felt as I were drunk as I attempted to step over the stretched out legs of a few Indian men sitting across the front entrance and drinking sweet tea. I tried to walk in a straight line down the *corniche* but my surroundings were all a blur, and it was all I could do to put one foot in front of the other. A little further, I spied a small café that specialized in juices and simple hamburgers and I headed inside.

I paid for two orders of French fries. As I leaned on my elbow – trying to keep my eyes open for ten long minutes – waiters flew up to the counter with dirty dishes before zipping off again with trays full of food. The cooks in the open kitchen were slapping together orders as fast as they could as loud Bollywood music kept up the tempo.

Back at the hotel, I rode up the rickety elevator and stumbled into our room. Adam and Nicholas were sitting in front of the television and I unceremoniously plunked the greasy bag of fries in front of them. As they noisily munched away, I started to wobble. As soon as I lay down on the bed, I fell asleep in my clothes for the fourth time in three days.

XXXIX. **I'm sitting by myself** in a bar that I've never been to before. The only other patrons are two men and two women seated on the opposite side of the room. They are drunk and swear a lot. I assume they are truck drivers – not because of the drinking and swearing, but more because they just have that look about them.

The bar features a pool table, a dartboard, and a coin-operated dispenser of roasted nuts. It's decorated almost exclusively with novelty tin signs that feature both the word 'beer' and at least one exclamation mark.

'Free Beer! Tomorrow!' reads one.

'Free Beer! Topless girls only!' reads another.

'Beer is the Answer! I just don't remember the question.'

'Everybody needs something to believe in. I believe I'll have another beer!'

I have to admit that I don't have high hopes for my burger.

*UPDATE: I was right about the burger. But the beer was good.*

XL. **I needed a good laugh** today, so I watched an episode of *Father Ted* – the mid-90s sitcom about three priests living on the fictional Craggy Island (off the west coast of Ireland). I've seen the episode called "Hell" about thirty-four times. It's ball-bouncingly funny.

The last time I traveled internationally, I watched the episode on the plane and kept everyone awake with my thunderous guffawing.

"I doubt very much that you made any new friends," said Paula when we landed. "You were *really* loud."

XLI. **The back of 7-Eleven** houses all sorts of weird and wonderful foods from the various dark corners of the planet. If one dares to go beyond the foot-long hot dogs that spin on rollers for days on end, or the 'free meat' that's pumped out of a half-clogged spout, then one can explore a plethora of prepackaged wonders with warning labels in foreign languages. One of these is a small unassuming bag of ridiculously spicy potato chips. 'It says spicy,' I thought, 'but really... how spicy can they be?'

I broke into the bag on the way home. And, rather than tentatively trying one chip and then another, I wolfed down seven in a row. This was a mistake. I began to sweat and my diaphragm started to spasm. I rushed home to fill my mouth with yogurt. I vowed never to do that again.

Naturally, I took them to school the next day.

It was shortly after lunchtime when my students were all quietly working on their short stories. Sometimes I work on my own writing during this time, but today I couldn't focus and wasn't sure what to do with myself. Maybe I was bored.

Bad things happen when I get bored – especially in the classroom.

"Hey, Stephen..." I whispered.

There was no response.

"Stephen."

Stephen stopped writing and looked up from his little white laptop.

"Do you want a chip?" I asked.

"Is there anything wrong with it?"

"No," I said. "You're really focused and doing an excellent job, and I was wondering if you'd like a small snack – as a reward."

"Okay."

It didn't take long before Stephen was frantically running around the classroom looking for something to dull the pain. I laughed and laughed.

I wonder if I'll get a phone call from his parents tomorrow.

XLII. **A joke that I've been telling** for the past thirty-two years: An older man is ice fishing, but isn't having any luck. Hours go by, and still he catches nothing. When he finally looks up from his spot on the lake, he spies another lone figure nearby.

The older man gets out of his chair and walks over for a bit of company. As he approaches, he notices that the lone figure is a young boy. Next to the young boy is a basket full of fish.

"My goodness," begins the older man. "Look at all these fish. Aren't you doing well? I haven't caught a thing. Tell me – if you don't mind – what is your secret?"

The young boy looks up and mumbles, "Yr hv ta kp yr wrms wm."

"Pardon me?" says the older man.

"Yr hv ta kp yr wrms wm."

The older man can't understand a word. "I'm sorry, my friend," he says, "but I didn't catch that. The wind is loud in my ears. Would you mind repeating yourself?"

"Yr hv ta kp yr wrms wm."

The older man takes off his toque, leans over, and cups his hands over his ears. "One more time, if you wouldn't mind."

The young boy spits a gob of something into his hand, looks up, and answers as loudly as he can. "You have to keep your worms warm!"

XLIII. **When asking** an Indigenous friend over for dinner I innocently asked, "Are you a red or white girl?"

I meant wine.

XLIV. **'In the same way** that pluralizing with an apostrophe has become the latest fashion trend in the systematic butchering of the English language,' I wrote in my journal last night, 'so too has the blatant overuse of the word 'literally' in casual conversation. I'm not sure why so many feel the need to use it so often, but it's abusive to the ears and should stop immediately.'

Paula and I had spent the night in Spokane after

attending a reading by David Sedaris. We went for a drink at the Sapphire Lounge before the show, and then another before bed. The staff is friendly and the artistic atmosphere is inviting.

We'd been there before. Sometimes we chat to each other as we sip our cocktails; sometimes we sit back and enjoy each other's company in silence.

With a signed copy of *Theft by Finding* sitting next to me, we finished the evening discussing various topics from pottery to empire penguins – until something caught my ear.

"I'm so hungry that I could *literally* eat a whole pie," said the young man sitting at the bar. "*Literally*, an entire lemon meringue pie."

It was difficult to determine the relationship between the young man and the lovely lady sitting next to him. Maybe they just met. Maybe they were old friends. Whatever the case, she didn't seem as put off by his language as she should have been.

"This is *literally* the best place to go for a drink, but there is *literally* no pie. If it were allowed, I would *literally* go into the kitchen and make a pie. That's how badly I want pie. Doesn't have to be lemon meringue. *Literally* any pie would do."

The young man's fixation on pie was strange, but not nearly as strange as his need to wedge the offending word into *literally* every sentence.

I told Paula that if this were a drinking game, I would be hammered in no time. I probably wouldn't make it up to our room.

XLV. **We hosted a dance troupe** at the school today. They showed the students some choreographed moves, and talked about teamwork and respect. But rather than participate or offer encouragement, I just wandered around the gymnasium making funny faces at the kindergarten kids.

XLVI. **You would think** that I'd learn. But in a rush to get to work on time, I forgot that I had left the windshield wipers on when I last turned off the car. As I started the engine with the door open and my leg hanging out, the wipers pushed off all the snow and most of it fell into my boot. Now I'm sitting in class, waiting for the school busses to arrive, with one wet sock.

XLVII. **I'll admit it:** I get lost easily. I have no sense of direction. Whether I am traveling by foot or by car, there are times when I have no idea where I am or how to get back from whence I came. Sometimes this weirds me out, and I get frustrated, and I want to just give up and never travel again. Other times, this leads to an adventure. And adventures are always worth it in the end.

I was constantly lost on my solo trip to Ireland. Which is funny now. It wasn't at the time.

After touring the archeological site of Newgrange, I decided that the best way to get from Brú na Bóinne to the town of Dingle – estimated at about four and half hours – was to head back towards Dublin and connect to the M50 before exiting onto the N7. While crossing the country, the N7 turns into the M7, which turns into the M20, which turns into the N21, and then finally turns into the N86 (because that's not confusing at all). If I didn't do anything silly, like stop for gas or anything to eat, I'd be in West Kerry for a nice cup of late-afternoon tea (and maybe a scone or a slice of pie).

With quick peeks at the coiled map book laid flat on the passenger seat, I tracked my progress every fifteen or twenty minutes. Traffic was busy, but that didn't bother me. Nor did driving on the opposite side of the road to what I was used to.

I tuned into RTÉ and a debate was raging on about water bills. Callers were complaining about having to pay, or having to pay more than they should. After an hour, I turned the dial to some traditional music – mostly fiddle and accordion tunes – and tapped on the steering wheel as the road wound on and on.

I passed exits for Rathcoole, Kilcullen, Kildare and Rathdowney – all places that would have to remain a mystery – and felt guilty for cruising across the country at a constant velocity without stopping to explore little villages along the way. But I had limited time in the country and little villages along the M7 would have to wait until another time.

The first couple hours went by without a hitch and I was confident I would reach Dingle by mid-afternoon. It was almost too easy. Crossing Ireland should involve have some sort of adventure, I thought. And that's when I noticed a posted detour.

A series of small signs directed me away from the highway, and down a series of country lanes. But soon there were only tall hedges and gnarly trees. The traffic had somehow thinned to nearly nothing.

"Perhaps I'll just continue on my way, find a local village, and there will be useful signs leading me back to where I need to go," I said to myself. I turned up the radio and vigorously drummed on the steering wheel to a rollicking fiddle tune.

I was driving more like a country Irishman than a cautious Canadian (which is never a good idea) as I flew over hills and around sharp corners. This reckless style can be excused if one is familiar with the lay of the land, but I wasn't. I didn't know, for instance, that I was about to approach a small village.

I sped right through it – far too fast to notice if there were useful signage. "I'll stop twice at the next village," I told myself.

After ten minutes of tall hedges and gnarly trees, there was another small village. This time I slowed down, hoping there was a welcome sign with the name of the village in clear lettering so I could reference it on my map. There wasn't.

The road split on the other side of this unnamed village. One road led uphill and the other road led downhill. I chose the one that led downhill. This was probably a mistake.

I was – without a doubt – ridiculously lost. On the rare occasion the road allowed me a quick peek at the map book, I tried to figure out where I was. No such luck. I could have been anywhere. Had Ireland not been an island, I may have been in another country.

Earlier, I had made a conscientious choice to turn down any sort of GPS or nav-sat features with my rental car. I considered it cheating. I wanted to welcome adventure as I explored the lesser-known Ireland.

However, having spent close to an hour driving all over hell's half-acre, I was beginning to see the appeal of modern-day technology.

The road suddenly came to an end, and I found myself on the edge of a town of some significant size. 'Maybe you should go looking for someone who could give us directions back to the highway,' said a voice of reason (from somewhere in the far reaches of my brain).

The first person I found was the local mechanic. He was wearing greasy overalls and was half-hidden under the hood of an old car.

"Excuse me," I said. "Um... I was wondering if you could tell me where I am."

The mechanic snorted and grumbled, and then straightened up and turned around. I was expecting him to be gruff and unpleasant but there was a big smile across his face. He still hadn't said anything.

"I was following this road," I continued, "but now I don't know where I am." I showed him the map book.

He scanned the page.

"Ah, right... well... this is a good map," he said. "But you're not on it."

"I'm not?" I asked as I looked down at the map.

"Not to worry," he laughed. "Here's what you got to do: head all the way through town and you'll see signs connecting you back to the motorway at the other end. It's very simple. Sure, you won't even need your map book."

He was right, and in ten minutes I was back on the highway. Soon enough I was skirting around Limerick and passing exits for Patrickswell, Newcastle West, and Knockgashel – more places that would have to remain a mystery.

As I approached Tralee – an hour from the town of Dingle – I decided to stretch my legs and find a gas station.

As I turned off the highway, I found the small arrow indicating what side the gas tank was on. But when I turned off the engine at the gas pump, I couldn't find the lever to release the gas cap door. It wasn't under the seat or under the dash. I popped the hood and the trunk (twice), and found the fuse box, but there was no gas lever.

"Excuse me," I said to a woman in her early-forties who was filling her sensible four-door sedan. "Have you any idea where the gas cap lever might be? I can't find it anywhere."

"Sorry," she said. "I don't. But you could try the lads inside. They might know."

They didn't know.

I decided to pry the gas cap door open with my car key, hoping not to cause too much damage, but it swiveled open as soon as I applied a little pressure with the palm of my hand. "That was a close call," I said to myself as I looked around to see if anyone had noticed.

I left Tralee without getting turned around (which was a huge success) and was on my way for the last fifty kilometers of the day's drive. The road was narrow and bumpy, and as I spied the Atlantic I fought to stay on the road as I admired the spectacular scenery.

It was then that I spotted a small sign pointing towards Inch Beach, and turned off the road somewhere between Camp and Annascaul. I thought it might be fun to go for a quick cup of tea and a bit of a walk before arriving at my final destination. Judging by the map book, there couldn't be more than ten kilometers separating the N86 from the southern edge of the peninsula. Inch Beach should be easy to find.

I got lost anyway. Time and space bent into some alternate universe as I drove around in circles. Every road was narrower than the last. Eventually there was a ridge on what seemed to be an animal trail. The road was barely wide enough for my rental car, and I got out at a little pullout to see if I could spy the beach. Instead, I found a muddy sheep.

Surprised to have a visitor, the sheep started running towards me. I wasn't sure if I should jump in the car and drive away before I was trampled, or attempt some form of communication. I chose the latter.

The sheep stopped and looked at me quizzically when it realized I was a stranger. But rather than turn around, the sheep stared at me and I stared back. With no one around to talk to, and my brain soft from driving across the country, I engaged the sheep in conversation. "Nice view," I said.

The sheep answered back, "Baa."

"You wouldn't happen to know the way to Dingle, would you?" I asked.

The sheep snorted in response.

This meant 'no'.

I got back into the car and continued up the hill. Luckily, half hidden behind an overgrown bush, there was a faded wooden sign directing me to town. I got lost a couple more times, but Dingle is a close-knit community and eventually I found someone who pointed me to where I needed to go.

I managed to get to my B&B just before sundown.

"What are your plans for this evening?" asked my host.

"I think a pint or two would be in order," I answered.

"Grand. From here you head down the hill..."

XLVIII. **Nicholas:** I whistled for the cat last night, and then... someone whistled back.

Me: Really?

Nicholas: Yeah. It was hilarious, but I thought I should lock the door.

Me: Good man.

XLIX. **"Our souls return** to this earth over a series of lifetimes," I read somewhere, "to evolve, learn, grow, transform, and become more spiritually attuned through the course of each life."

I wonder sometimes if I returned this time around – as a somewhat befuddled teacher – to learn about school alarm systems.

It was shortly after lunch that I decided to light the birthday candles for a colleague's cake directly under a smoke detector.

Despite my best efforts to let them know that everything was okay, the fire department arrived anyway.

L. **Up until yesterday,** I was adamant that weaving through the endless labyrinth of IKEA on a Sunday afternoon was not for me. I'd rather wait outside a Victoria's Secret store with nothing to read. Or compare paint swatches for the feature wall in our living room.

But as we turned off the highway, and searched for a spot at the far end of the parking lot, I decided that I would at least play the role of supporting husband and try to appear interested. As expected, I failed within a matter of minutes.

As Paula was focused at creating a new kitchen with the help of several employees and a grubby computer, I got bored. And, after slipping away like a hallway ninja, I wandered off to observe other shoppers. One young couple argued about everything. A teenage girl climbed to the upper bunk in a display bedroom. An older gentleman mumbled something about the outside world and fresh air. I thought about placing my hand on his shoulder and offering my support, but I didn't. Instead I played with the light switches. I stole three golf pencils. I attempted to juggle toilet brushes.

All sense of time and place melted away as colours and shapes blurred into a wide spectrum of names I couldn't pronounce. Dreaming of a time before I entered the doors into Wonderland, I came across yet another bedroom mock-up. An attractive woman in her thirties was splayed out, testing the mattress.

'That looks like fun,' I thought.

I didn't say, "That looks like fun." I just thought it.

But she must have read my mind, because she looked up and made bedroom eyes at me. 'Come over here, you fine fellow,' she seemed to say with her emerald green eyes.

The fight-or-flight response (also called hyper-arousal, or the acute stress response) is a physiological reaction that occurs in response to a perceived harmful event, attack, or threat to survival.

Perhaps, in this case, another 'F' word should be added to that list.

I wish I were a fight kind-of guy. But I'm not. Embarrassing as it is to admit, I am the other kind-of guy. I'm a run-back-into-the-house-with-my-cat kind-of guy.

Having completed an awkward triple take, and becoming flushed in the face, I did not jump in bed with her, make some suave remark, and give her a quick snog.

Instead, I froze.

And the voices in my head started arguing.

'Maybe she was winking at her husband,' thought one.

'We should slowly turn around and check,' thought another.

'God, how embarrassing would it be to jump in bed with her,' thought a third voice, 'only for her husband to clear his throat – or worse, start laughing and pointing. Can you imagine?'

There was no one behind me.

'Now what are we supposed to do?' questioned yet another voice. 'We can't just awkwardly stare.'

I wish I could write that a voice of reason emerged from the cacophony of noise in my head. But I can't.

I wish I could write that I winked and smiled, and flexed my pectorals. Or something equally manly. But I can't.

Instead, I booted it. And found my wife.

"You're not going to believe what just happened," I said to Paula a few minutes later.

She laughed so hard that many of the customers stopped what they were doing to look over.

"How are you going to write about this? You should go back and see what happens."

"What!? I can't go back."

"Your readers will be left wondering."

By the time I found the bed again, it was empty.

No awkward snog, but a whole different appreciation for IKEA.

## About The Author

Chris Brauer lives in southeastern British Columbia, where he splits his time between teaching and writing. He enjoys traveling, eating out, arguing with his cats, and wearing wool sweaters. He composes on a filthy laptop, edits with a Visconti fountain pen, and posts random musings on social media. Currently, Chris is working on a number of projects – both prose and poetry – when he's not loading the dishwasher or figuring out how to fold fitted sheets.

## Follow Chris Brauer

https://www.facebook.com/chrisbrauerwriter

https://www.instagram.com/chrisbrauer.writer

www.chrisbrauerwriter.com

Made in the USA
Monee, IL
23 December 2020

55476810R00046